Mary H. C. Booth

Wayside Blossoms

Mary H. C. Booth

Wayside Blossoms

ISBN/EAN: 9783744652940

Printed in Europe, USA, Canada, Australia, Japan

Cover: Foto ©Thomas Meinert / pixelio.de

More available books at **www.hansebooks.com**

Wayside Blossoms.

Wayside Blossoms

BY

Mary H. C. Booth.

PHILADELPHIA.
J. B. LIPPINCOTT & CO.
1865.

Entered, according to Act of Congress, in the year 1865,

By J. B. LIPPINCOTT & CO.

In the Clerk's Office of the District Court for the Eastern District of Pennsylvania.

Contents.

	PAGE
The Angel Post	9
The Echo of the Alps	10
Forever Thine	12
At the Golden Gate	14
The Pilgrim's Pillow	15
Coming, Love	17
O, Annie May	18
The dear old Robin Red-breast	19
A Little Blossom	22
A Mountain Monument	25
The Beautiful Gem on the Way	29
The Volunteer's Vision	30
I shall be with Thee	32
The Broken Band	34
Willie Brown	37
Poems Unwritten	39
Send me some Little Token	40
The Western Woods	41

CONTENTS.

	PAGE
"While God He leaves me Reason, God He will leave me Jim"	45
The Western Volunteer	48
A Kingly Heritage	52
We Met and Parted	55
Beat to her Pulses Sweet	57
Eva	58
Too Late	60
Lulu Bell	61
Bella Dowe	63
Sweet Bessie Gray	65
Heart Breathings	66
Good Night	68
Tossed upon Life's Heaving Ocean	69
I will not say Good-bye	70
The Alpine Lovers	71
I'm Dying, Comrade	74
The Lord will Make it Good	76
I saw Thee from Afar	78
Our Little Bird of Paradise	79
To William Cullen Bryant, on his Seventieth Birthday	81
Angels! Lead Her Lightly	83
The Old Year	84
The New Year	85
Our Souls leap over the Years	86
Thine at Last	89
Allie Grey	90

CONTENTS.

	PAGE
The Swiss Peasant Woman's Offering to the Sanitary Fair	92
Jack and Jim, Comrades, who fell at the Battle of Fort Fisher	94
Good Friday	99
The Dead Boy	100
The Twin Baby Sleepers	102
"It might have been"	103
Song of the Rhine	104
Let the Angels be my Guide	105

Wayside Blossoms.

The Angel-Post.

I HAVE nothing to say to you, dearest—
  Nothing that I can write,
For all the word that I had to send,
  I sent by the Post to-night.

Not in the form of a letter,
  With mark and stamp and seal,
Did I trust the tender message
  That my soul had to reveal.

Not in a bunch of blossoms,
  Not in a sweet bouquet,
Did I hide the beautiful meaning,
  Of the words I dared not say.

But I sent the sweet heart-music
  No mortal on Earth ere wrote,
What need that the soul's soft melodies
  Be written down by note?

So I've nothing to say to you, dearest,
  But to send you my love at most,
And the news of my heart that I cannot write,
  I send by the Angel-Post.

The Echo of the Alps.

MY heart is wandering to the West,
  With swift and noiseless flight,
To seek its eagle in his nest,
And pluck a feather from his breast
  Beneath the wings of night —
A feather from his beating breast
  That shall my song indite,
A feather from his wounded breast
  With which my soul may write.

    Hush! for I feel a flutter —
      As if my pen possessed
    The wizard power to utter
      The thoughts within my breast.

THE ECHO OF THE ALPS.

I soar above the glaciers' gleam,
  I am the night-bird's guest,
I fly with him o'er storm and stream,
And never pause, and dream my dream,
  And seek my ark of rest.

Thou art where flowery prairies roll,
  But thy heart is on the wing,
And the mellow music of thy soul
  Gives answer as I sing.
Thou hast called the whirlwind for a guide
  Across the sounding sea,
And the spirit of the wind replied
  That his rushing wings were free.

I viewed thee from the Alpine height
  In the chamois' agile bound,
And felt thee in the lark's delight,
  And in the torrent's sound.
I heard thee in the tempest's tone,
  And in the rippling rills,
I saw thee in the woodlands lone,
  And called thee from the hills.

And the very heavens resounded
  With the music of thy name,
And the listening Alps rebounded
  In fiery floods of flame.

And the spirit of the Alps replied,
  That he felt thy dauntless soul
In the fearless avalanche's slide,
  And in the thunder's roll.

He told me that thy spirit's home
  Was on his glancing towers,
And in his torrent's sparkling foam,
  And in the Alpine flowers.

And a voice beyond the golden stars
  Proclaimed thy dwelling there —
I hold thee in my prison bars,
  Yet thou art everywhere.

Forever Thine.

"FOREVER thine!" O, simple words!
  Ye lift my soul on charmèd wings,
And waken all its silent birds,
  That have not sung so many springs.

Those simple words, "forever thine"—
  A letter's sweet and lingering close,
With deep and double under-line,
  Stained with the soft leaves of a rose.

FOREVER THINE.

'Tis many months, and may be, years,
   Since the dear letter's words were penned;
I've read them through so many tears,
   I scarce can read them more, dear friend.

And yet the tears are not of pain,
   Nor all of joy, for while I weep
I read "forever thine" again,
   And dream — forever mine — in sleep.

I know not why I inly sing
   At those sweet words, "forever thine" —
As if the spirit of the spring
   Had brought them meaning more divine.

This morning, as I read them o'er,
   The tear-stained letters seemed to shine!
And one who was of earth no more
   Retraced the dear "forever thine."

At the Golden Gate.

"OH DON'T you remember" the corn, Bell Blair!
    That waved in the Autumn breeze,
Like the peaceful flow of a mother's prayer,
    Or the swell of the singing seas?
And how, when the harvest time came on,
    We hid in its golden sheaves
To watch for the coming of gentle John,
    From under the low barn eaves?

I am not ashamed that I loved John Dean,
    For his heart was pure and true,
Though the flowers he culled in the spring-time
    green
    Were always given to you.
And you crushed them under your feet, Bell Blair!
    As he lovingly turned away;
But I gathered them up to my heart, and there
    They are all a-bloom to-day.

Ah, well I remember the roses, born
    With his beautiful love for thee —
How he freed their stems of the faintest thorn,
    And the briers were given to me.

They are all I shall ever ask, Bell Blair!
    But I know my brier will bloom
To a fragrant flower for my soul to wear,
    For I smell its rich perfume.

Sometimes, when the shadowy mist uncurls
    From the path my soul will tread,
And the rose unfolds mid the eddying whirls
    Of the snow around my head.
And now, when the harvest time comes on
    In heaven, I shall gladly wait,
And watch for the coming of angel John,
    At the beautiful golden gate.

The Pilgrim's Pillow.

PITY me, loving Lord!
    Thou, who on Earth hadst not a place of rest,
    The sparrow has his nest,
And I — I have Thy Word.

In the world's wilderness alone I stand,
    Yet not alone, O God!
I walk beneath the shelter of Thy hand,
    And kiss Thy chastening rod.

I seek among the brambles for a spot
   Whereon to lay my aching heart and head
But find no place, yet I have not forgot,
   How Thy beloved are led.

I know that in the world's deep wilderness,
   The crystal waters of Thy mercies flow,
But we are blinded by our small distress,
   And think too seldom on Thy sacred woe.

I sought a downy spot, but there was none,
   Save in the fragrant bloom of thistle-down,
My softest pillow is a mossy stone —
   Thistles were better than my Saviour's crown.

Unbidden tears come welling to my eyes,
   And yet I know He watched me while I slept;
The little larks with sweetest prayers arise,
   And I remember that my Jesus wept!

It was not Want, nor simple suffering,
   Nor, that the brambles wounded by the way,
That caused the sorrow of the Shepherd King —
   His lambkins went astray.

It matters little, if the weary way
   Be long or short, or flowery, straight or steep,
For well I know that in His own good day
   He giveth all of His beloved sleep.

Coming, Love!

I HEAR the rustle of the leaves,
   I see a shadow glide
From the sweet stillness of the eves
   When we were side by side,
   And all the world was wide —
And we were all the world, mine own,
Its joy, and melody, and moan,
Until there crept an under-tone,
And swelled to this deep dirge — alone!

Thy shadow, Love! is coming
   Across the weary years;
My heart is faintly humming
   A song thy name endears.

It almost breaks to listen —
   I feel thy tread so still,
And all the dewdrops glisten,
   And all the roses thrill;
And all the blessed angels
   Are smiling from above,
And singing sweet evangels,
   For thou art coming, Love!

O, Annie May!

'TWAS Summer in the sunny West
    When first I met you by the way;
'T is little I have known of rest —
    Ah! little, since that sunny day.

Why were you there, O, Annie May!
    With song-birds hopping on your breast
No wonder they should love to play
    Around so beautiful a nest.

Were you a-weary, Annie May!
    Of what, and whom, O, sweetest maid!
Or wherefore was it that you lay
    Asleep beneath the hazel shade?

I saw you in the noonday hours,
    With these black eyes that cannot see;
I thought you were a bunch of flowers —
    Of snow-white blossoms blown for me.

Was there no angel in the West
    To stoop and tell you I was there —
To start the song-birds from your breast.
    And send them singing up in air?

No spirit of the wood-land dell
   To turn my weapon's aim away?
The dead and bleeding birdling fell,
   And thou — alas! O, Annie May!

O, Annie May! O, Annie May!
   Could I have seen thee once before,
Perhaps 't were not so hard to say
   That I shall see thee now no more.

And may be it were harder still —
   I cannot say: I can but weep,
As here, upon a daisied hill,
   I sit and guard thy dreamless sleep.

The dear old Robin Red-breast.

I WAKENED as the lark went up, at daylight's
    early dawning,
To bid the Angels up in heaven a jubilant good
    morning,
A thousand loving little larks were singing in my
    breast,
But the grand old robin red-breast sang louder than
    the rest.

He sang from out the dear old years through memory's golden vista,
I saw him sitting on the birch beside his pretty sister,
The same as when in other morns we watched their sober plays.
I dreamed of you last night, Bob! of the robins and the jays;

And of the sweet witch-hazel, and of the four-leaved clover,
And of our castles in the air that long since tumbled over;
And of the fragrant sassafras, and of the scented fern,
O, Bob! if all those blessed days could once again return!

If I could have a spikenard root, or smell the wintergreen,
Or pluck the lustrous princess-pine, or see the laurel's sheen —
Why, I should almost feel, dear Bob! as if, with hand in hand,
We wandered through the spicy woods, in the bright old summer-land.

Have you kept the long brown curl, Bob! I gave
 you when we parted?
I've never lost your golden lock, but you were
 giddy hearted,
And it may be that you have thrown the worthless
 thing away —
Was it a worthless thing to you? perhaps — I cannot say.

Last week I read of you, dear Bob! in Harper's
 Magazine,
It seems that you are Bob no more, but Captain
 Robert Green;
It may be you are Captain, or a General — may be,
But never anything but Bob can you ever be to me.

I read about how brave you were, and of your good
 promotion,
And then I kissed the sunny lock whose mates are
 o'er the ocean;
And all last night I dreamed of you, and the robin
 hopped between,
And sang unto my heart of Bob — not Captain
 Robert Green.

A Little Blossom.

TO GERRIT SMITH.

I DARE not speak of thee, in idle rhyming,
    As one might of another,
Thou, whose great soul with all things good is
       chiming,
    The world's most loving brother!

Thou, in whose heart the most melodious measures
    Keep sweetest tune and time;
Yet I have nought, from all my little treasures,
    To give thee, but my rhyme.

For when my heart, with beautiful emotion,
    Is lifted high and higher,
Thrilled with thy thoughts, from o'er the Alps and
       ocean,
    As with electric fire —

It is but meet to find some sweet oblation,
    With reverence to bring
Unto thy feet, thou living revelation
    Of what the mountains sing!

And I have nothing save a little blossom,
  Gathered beneath the snow,
Upon St. Gothard's palpitating bosom,
  Where Alpine roses blow.

Beyond a thousand dimpling dells and fountains
  I see the glaciers gleam;
O'er the white vesture of the Alpine mountains
  Eternal rainbows beam.

I look — the hills are towering in the distance,
  Where the immortal Three
Swore a great oath that with the Lord's assistance,
  Their country should be free.

And the Alps heard it, while at their foundations
  The very roses smiled —
They thought how God had given to the nations
  The Freedom they defiled.

Therefore a little Alpine flower I find thee —
  A messenger of light,
Unfolden on the mountains, to remind thee
  It is not always night.

The buds of Freedom through thy spirit breaking,
   Begin to burst in bloom;
And Liberty shall have her full awaking,
   O'er Slavery's tearless tomb.

Thy life has been a beautiful evangel
   To all the weak and lowly;
For the oppressed thou art a guardian angel,
   A psalter high and holy.

The soul of Switzerland upsprings to meet thee,
   She stretches out her hand
Across the mountains and the seas to greet thee,
   And lure thee to her land.

   Zurich, Switzerland.

A Mountain Monument.*

TO GENERAL GARIBALDI.

GARIBALDI imprisoned! And yet the hills
   Are as free as they were at morn,
And a mountain soul in fetters — God!
   The Alps grow pale with scorn!

They think of the gleam of the first sunbeam,
   When the wakening world was young,
When the little hills lay down to dream,
   And the stars of the Morning sung.

And of how, at the sound of the Freedom song,
   They rose up into space,
And stood by the side of the starry throng
   And looked God in the face.

---

* There is a gigantic formation of Alps — comprising part of the Bernina Range — in the Upper Engadine, Switzerland, bearing the lineaments of a human face — recently noted for its striking resemblance to Garibaldi, the news of whose wounds and imprisonment at Aspromonte, reached us while sojourning at Pontresina, in sight of this marvellous creation.

They listened with their regal forms
    Upheld in royal might,
And heard above the chaos storms,
    His sweet, "Let there be light!"

The mountains crimsoned with delight,
    And shook in thunder thrills;
They leaned across the jeweled night,
    And whispered to the hills.

And the little hills upspringing,
    Gave back an answering nod,
Then burst out into singing
    Of Freedom and of God.

And Freedom took her dwelling place
    Upon the mountains fair,
And proudly, with a goddess' grace,
    She rocks her eagles there.

The mountains shivered with unrest,
    The pitying goddess smiled,
She saw upon their snowy breast
    The picture of her child.

Thy picture, Garibaldi!
    Upon the hills of God!
Where tyrant monarch never reigned,
    And Despot never trod.

A MOUNTAIN MONUMENT.

She saw its towering forehead rise
   An Alp, with sun-lit snows!
Beneath its rainbow-archèd eyes
   She heard the storms repose —

The storm-winds breathing low and deep,
   And whispering in their dreams,
As when a giant speaks in sleep,
   On most melodious themes.

Around its bearded granite mouth
   She saw the fringe of pines —
The sighing pine trees leaning South
   And swaying toward the vines.

She saw its glorious features turned
   To the sweet land of song,
And her majestic spirit spurned
   The world that wrought him wrong.

She longed to lure the Poet Land
   Up to her crystal throne —
To lead her by the rosy hand
   Where Freedom reigns alone.

She longed to bid her dauntless sons
   Rise in imperial might,
And lift her loved and fettered ones
   Up to her realm of light.

The indignant eagles sunward start;
  The wondering winds awake —
Freedom is wounded in the heart
  For all her children's sake.

At Garibaldi's prison bars,
  The guardian goddess sings!
She lifts the blood-stained "Stripes and Stars"
  Over the thrones of kings!

Enthroned on the Eternal hills,
  With God within her sight,
She hears the nation's tocsin-thrills,
  And feels a Conqueror's might.

She sees her glorious Flag unfurled
  To every Nation's breath;
Her clarion war-cry for the World
  Is "Liberty or Death!"

The Beautiful Gem on the Way.

I KNOW a sweet letter is winging
   Its way, o'er the land and the sea,
And a beautiful burden is bringing,
   From over the hills, to me.

I know how the glad spirit fluttered,
   When it thrilled to the words that were penned,
Yet the beautiful thoughts unuttered,
   Are those I most wish her to send.

She wrote with a tremulous shiver,
   And wondered whene'er we should meet
This side of the murmuring river,
   Where sweet shall be mingled with sweet.

I would that I were but the blushes,
   That smiled on her out of the east,
Or even a pause in the hushes,
   Where her musical breathing had ceased.

I know only this of the letter —
   I dreamed she had written to me
My spirit is bound with a fetter
   From which I would never be free.

I will patiently wait till the coming
  Of the beautiful gem on the way,
While my spirit is inwardly humming
  The words that I know she will say.

The Volunteer's Vision.

LAST night as I lay in the rain,
  And looked up to heaven through the night,
A vision came o'er me, and lighted my brain
With a glory that never will flood it again,
  This side of the River of Light.

And I heard a sweet sound as it came,
  Like the flutter of feathery wings,
And the voice of a seraph kept calling my name,
And her breath in my tresses went playing the same
  As the air in an instrument's strings.

I told my wild heart to be still,
  That the vision was naught but a dream,
For I knew not that over the amethyst hill
The feet of my darling had wandered at will,
  On the banks of Eternity's stream.

THE VOLUNTEER'S VISION.   31

I said to the seraph-winged bird,
  O, why have you come from the West?
And she told how the leaves of the forest were
    stirred
By the feet of the angels who brought her the
    word
  Of a land where the weary may rest.

She said she was tired and faint,
  And her heart was all covered with snow;
The angels they heard her unuttered complaint,
They called her, and brought her the robes of a
    saint,
  And she said she was ready to go.

I told her the blossoms were sweet,
  In the meadows, the same as of yore;
But she showed me the dew on her sparkling feet,
They had caught of the lilies that bordered the
    street,
  By the sands of the Paradise shore.

I asked her how long I must wait
  Before I should meet her afar,
And I prayed her unfold me the book of my fate;
But she vanished, and passed through the crystal-
    line gate
  She had left in her coming ajar.

Dear Hugh, there's a battle to-day,
  And perchance I may happen to fall;
If I'm not at the call of the roll, you may say
A good-bye to the boys in my name, for I may
  Have said "aye" to an Angel's call.

I shall be with Thee.

I HEAR a footstep in the hall,
  I see a shadow on the wall —
A moving shadow dark and tall —
A voiceless shadow — this is all.

No gentle footfall near my door
Thrills to my heart across the floor,
And I am weary thinking o'er
That music I shall hear no more —

That tender music, soft, and sweet —
The melody of coming feet;
I cry, and echo sends the call
Back to my heart — and this is all.

I SHALL BE WITH THEE.

I feel a soft hand on my head —
A hand whose touch seems overspread
With balm, like that the lilies shed
O'er the white bosoms of the dead;
And I am chill, while memories fall
Like odors o'er me — this is all.

I feel the rhythm and the rhyme
Of thy dear life keep sweetest time
With God's sweet sounds, and overclimb
All sounds with which they inter-chime.
I see thee — hear thee — feel thy breath
In the still air which answereth,
With lightest kiss whene'er I call,
Mid tears for thee — and this is all.

I cannot hear thee in the hall,
Nor see thy shadow on the wall,
Yet I shall hear an angel call
My name adown the jasper wall;
For when the leaves of Autumn fall,
I shall be with thee — this is all.

The Broken Band.

COME o'er the sea, dear friend, with me,
    Back to the good old days,
No need to-night of other light —
    The maple log's a-blaze.
So let it burn, while we return,
    And by its pleasant glow
We'll walk the ways, and sing the lays
    Of the dear old long-ago.

I'll sit here in the shadow, but you must have the light;
For I would see your soul shine out upon your face to-night.
You will listen for sweet voices, and you think I cannot hear,
So tell your dear old secrets and forget that I am near.

I'll sit here while you're talking with the forms I cannot see,
Perhaps I feel their presence, though they never think of me;
I see a gleam of silver above the old arm-chair,
And a sound like one of David's psalms is floating in the air.

Here sat the grand old patriarch and patriot, whose
    tone
Once floated from the old arm-chair up to the golden
    throne;
And there, beside the long great clock, I seem to
    see a gleam,
So like an angel's crown of light, it cannot be a
    dream.

And underneath the saintly crown I see a silver
    head —
I know the blessed grandame sleeps beside the
    dreamless dead;
And yet she sits there singing, with her knitting in
    her hand,
A song from Watts his hymn book about the Better
    Land.

There enters at the open door the stately country
    squire,
With the pretty maid who sang the best of all the
    village choir;
Why do you start and turn away at her still foot-
    step's fall?
Ah, me! I hear your whispered vows, and then —
    an angel's call.

I know the Squire is Colonel now, in the brave New
    Hampshire ranks;
Was he the gallant Colonel Brown who fought with
    General Banks?
"Yes; and a glorious fellow he — he'll have a grand
    career"—
Poor friend, I lay the Times aside — the Colonel's
    death is here.

I'll not disturb your reverie with talking of the
    brave —
The cottage boundaries expand — I stand beside a
    grave:
"I wonder where my brother Will is wandering to-
    night?"
Dear Willie walks the pearly streets up in the
    realms of light.

I heard the soldier's funeral hymn they chanted
    o'er his rest,
I saw them fold the glorious Flag above his dream-
    less breast,
And I see him standing, even now, beside you,
    while you speak,
With golden curls upon his brow, and smiles upon
    his cheek.

Come o'er the main, dear friend, again,
  Back, to the Alpine Land;
Thy household door shall ope no more
  On an unbroken band.
The loving lays of other days
  By Angel lips are sung,
And others walk the flowery ways
  We trod when we were young.

Willie Brown.

THE night was dark in Ireland,
  The rain was falling down,
And death was stealing to the heart
  Of little Willie Brown.

He lay upon his mother's knee,
  And looked within her eyes;
Of summers he had known but three,
  And they were three of sighs.

He looked within her gentle eyes
  And tried in vain to speak;
And paler grew the faded flowers
  Upon his lily cheek.

And well the mother knew the words
  Her darling would have said,
For there he lay a-dying —
  Dying for want of bread.

The rain upon the grassy roof
  Came wildly rushing down,
And angels waited for the soul
  Of little Willie Brown.

He lay upon his mother's knee,
  And faster fell the rain;
He never looked within her eyes,
  Or asked for bread again.

And paler grew his lily cheek,
  His golden hair uncurled,
And the angels whispered him away
  From hunger and the world.

Poems Unwritten.

THERE are poems unwritten, and songs unsung,
   Sweeter than any that ever were heard —
Poems that wait for an angel tongue,
   Songs that but long for a Paradise bird.

Poems that ripple through lowliest lives —
   Poems unnoted and hidden away
Down in the souls where the beautiful thrives,
   Sweetly as flowers in the airs of the May.

Poems that only the angels above us,
   Looking down deep in our hearts, may behold —
Felt, though unseen, by the beings who love us,
   Written on lives as in letters of gold.

Sing to my soul the sweet song that thou livest!
   Read me the poem that never was penned —
The wonderful idyl of life that thou givest
   Fresh from thy spirit, O, beautiful friend!

Send me Some Little Token.

SEND me some little token,
    That my yearning heart may know
That the vows have not been broken,
    Of the beautiful long ago.

I can feel in the twilight chilly,
    Whenever I think of thee,
The soul of the fragrant lily,
    Quietly steal o'er me—

Drowning my sense so sweetly
    In a flood of pure perfume,
That thy presence fills completely
    The air of my quiet room.

Send me a sprig that has pattered
    In the wind on thy window pane,
Where the wrens in the morn have chattered
    To the sound of the running rain.

Send me a leaf or a blossom
    That thy beautiful eyes have seen,
With a sigh from thy heart to my bosom,
    To quietly creep between.

It will come like a balm to the wounded,
    And shiver the rock in twain,
Where the bark of my hope is grounded,
    In the surge of the tossing main.

The Western Woods.

I CANNOT see the glittering Alps that sparkle on my sight,
I gaze upon their snowy peaks, but on another light:
I look beyond the haze of years, to the Indian Summer days,
And I see the boundless prairies of the Western world a-blaze!

I hear the crackling of the fire, upon the distant breeze,
The soft and rosy atmosphere comes dreaming o'er the seas —
The balmy Indian Summer air that mellows all the West,
And lays the Autumn's drapery upon the Winter's breast.

The magic of the hazy air has borne me back again
To the cabin by the maple grove, beside the prairie
    plain;
I sit within the long, dry grass, and watch the
    untravelled way,
And I see my pretty little fawns, under the oaks,
    at play.

The lovely creatures spring aside, and dart across
    the grass,
And then I hear a footstep near—I'll wait, and let
    it pass;
And so I fold my trembling hands across my half-
    shut eyes,
But it cannot close the vision out between me and
    the skies.

"You came so still, dear neighbor Phil, you set my
    heart a-flutter;"
And this was all that I recall 'twas possible to
    utter;
I wished the creeping twilight tide on fleeter wings
    had sped,
And this was what I thought about, but I know not
    what I said.

But this I know, the sunset's glow had made my
    pale cheek rosy,
I feared the flush was like a blush, I stooped and
    plucked a posy;
'Twas but a faded prairie flower, and neighbor
    Philip smiled,
"Oh, come," said he, "and walk with me, the airs
    are soft and mild."

We wandered to a woodland stream, and heard a
    wild swan sing,
We saw a flock of pigeons soar above us on the
    wing;
We heard the whirring partridge pass, and startled
    up a roe,
Yet how we came to frighten her is more than I
    can know.

We never could have talked aloud — I know not if
    at all —
You might have heard a breathing bird, or the
    lightest leaflet's fall;
I think that Philip did not speak, and yet it really
    seems
As if some low-toned words of his were woven in
    my dreams.

It must have been his eyes that spoke — 't was nothing but his eyes —
A roe might just as well have run from the starlight of the skies;
Yet I remember, while I think, of how I tried to hide,
As I felt him coming through the grass, in the early even-tide.

We stepped across a babbling brook, the wild-duck were asleep
Among the fragrant water-flowers, in slumbers soft and deep.
How lovely it must be to rest in such a wild-wood bed,
With silver sands beneath the feet, and the stars of heaven o'erhead.

We heard the prairie-chickens peep from out their hidden nest;
'T was time that they were fast asleep, 'neath their mother's speckled breast;
And though the early stars were out, we heard the whistling quail;
Were I to tell of all we heard, my pen and ink would fail.

And yet the loudest sound of all was in each throbbing breast,
My heart has never ceased to beat with the same sweet wild unrest;
And now the Alpine Autumn leaves are rustling on the ground,
But I only see the Western Woods, and hear my own heart's sound.

"While God He leaves me Reason God He will leave me Jim."*

"SOLDIER! say, did you meet my Jimmy in the fight?
You'd know him by his manliness, and by his eyes' sweet light."
"I fought beside your gallant son — a brave, good fellow he;
Alas! he fell beneath the shot that should have taken me."

* Words of an American soldier's mother, who, on hearing that her son had fallen in battle, became hopelessly insane, though continually insisting that his having "fallen" was of no consequence.

"And think you that my Jimmy cared about a
    little fall?
Why make a great ado of what he would not mind
    at all?
When Jimmy was a little boy and played with
    Bobby Brown,
He always played the enemy, and Bob he shot him
    down.

"I've seen him fall a hundred times — the cunning
    little sprite!
He can't forget his boyish tricks, though in an
    earnest fight.
But never mind about the fall, I want to hear of
    him;
Perhaps you've heard the Captain speak of what he
    thinks of Jim?"

"I often heard the Captain say, Jim was a splendid
    lad —
The bravest, and the handsomest, of all the boys
    he had;
And here's a lock of Jimmy's hair, and here's a
    golden ring —
I found it tied around his neck upon a silken
    string."

The mother took the matted tress, she took the ring of gold,
But shook her head, and laughed aloud at what the soldier told:
"Soldier!" said she, "where is my boy — Where is my brave boy Jim?
I gave the others all to God, but God He left me him.

"Hush! there is Uncle Abraham, a-knocking at the door,
He calls for other mother's sons — three hundred thousand more!
Be still, Old Uncle Abraham — 't will do no good to call;
You think my house is full of boys — ah! Jimmy was my all!"

The Western Volunteer.

I KNEW his loyal heart would leap at the first battle sound,
And that his glorious soul would spring with wild exultant bound,
To meet the traitors face to face, upon the traitor-land;
The sound of his melodious voice will quell the rebel band,
The thunder of his glorious voice will shake the despot's sand.

His very words to other boys are as a trumpet's call;
The widow Alden's sons are brave, but mine is most of all.
And sister Jane, whose Samuel has quite a fair renown,
Told me this morning that my John was the bravest boy in town,
And she said that John was fit to die, like the Patriot John Brown.

I told her I could keep the sun from sinking in the
  West,
As well as I could keep my John within the house-
  hold nest;
For ever since the darling knew of Sumpter's fear-
  less fate,
It seems as if the blessed boy was almost filled with
  hate —
The South will soon begin to wish there was no
  Western State.

I've nothing in the world to say against an Eastern
  lad,
For Dick was born at home in Maine, and Dick is
  not so bad;
Yet brother Richard never was the boy that John
  will be;
There may be other lads as good, but John's the
  best for me
Of all the boys that go to war — we'll see what we
  shall see!

As I was telling sister Jane ('t was natural, you
  know),
I almost thought my heart would break, when I
  knew that John would go;

But I never said a single word, except that he was
 right,
Yet I believe my hands they shook, as I handed
 him the light
Before he went up stairs to bed to his little room
 that night.

I sat beside the kitchen fire, and thought about
 my son;
It cannot be that I was weak — he is my only one —
But I never dreamed of keeping him ('t would be
 of no avail),
I thought how true the boy would be if all the rest
 should fail;
If John was set against the World, the World could
 not prevail.

I took the candle from the stand, and softly went
 up stairs,
As when, in other days, I heard my baby say his
 prayers;
But John was sleeping, and I laid my hand upon
 his head;
What was it that the blessed boy in his sweet sleeping said?
Poor child! 'twas not his mother's name, but a
 maiden's name instead.

I kissed his lips, and kissed his cheek, and smoothed
    his clustering hair;
O, what a glorious boy he was as he lay dreaming
    there;
I thought what Gen. Scott would think, to see so
    brave a man
Come thundering from the Western States, the
    foremost in the Van;
The good old General shall see that what we will,
    we can!

If there should be a rebel Flag flaunting within
    the town,
My John he is the very boy to go and take it
    down.
My sister asked how I should feel if John should
    chance to fall?
Ah! such a thing could never be — I have no fear
    at all;
I tell you John is proof against the fleetest cannon-
    ball.

The prairie and the village street thrill to the drum
    and fife;
I could not help these truant tears, were it to save
    my life.

The cars are starting for the East amid a thousand
    cheers;
Though mother of a soldier son, I cannot stay my
    tears.
God bless the noble regiments of Western Volun-
    teers!

A Kingly Heritage.

I HAVE a little drop of blood
    Whose course is wild and fleet,
Sometimes I feel it in my soul,
    And sometimes in my feet.
Sometimes it courses like a rill,
    And sometimes like a flood,
And often I am deluged with
    This little drop of blood.

I know from whence the heritage —
    From out the hearts of kings —
Sometimes it grows ethereal,
    And spreads itself in wings;
And then I feel the souls of winds
    Go bearing me away
Back to the high ancestral halls,
    Where jewelled fountains play.

A KINGLY HERITAGE.

Within the royal temple's aisles
    Divinest singers sing,
And at the holy altar shrines
    The sweetest censers swing,
The incense of whose pure perfume
    Melts through the azure dome,
And forms again in spirit flowers,
    In the "Mighty Spirit's" home.

The crowns that graced the haughty brows
    Of my ancestral kings,
Were not of yellow gold and stones,
    But glorious eagle's wings.
Their palace halls — the boundless woods,
    Their shrines — the forest bowers,
Their singers — all the birds of heaven,
    Their censer cups — the flowers.

The temples that they worshipped in,
    They were not made with hands,
And they had their hunting grounds of One
    Who never sells His lands.
And when the mighty buffalo,
    With their majestic tread,
Went shaking down the stars from heaven,
    From the hunting grounds o'erhead,

The Brave, to whom the spirit spake,
  Replied with regal pride,
And with his death-song on his lips
  He laid him down and died.
Ye sleep, O, kingly ancestors!
  Beneath the forest trees,
But your royal ghosts are still about
  Upon the woodland breeze.

Sometimes they tramp across my heart
  As through a hunting ground;
I feel a hundred Indians leap
  Within it at a bound.
'Tis but a little drop of blood,
  And yet I feel it roll
As if a thousand tomahawks
  Were lifted in my soul!

It lights the secret council fires
  Within my heart and brain,
At which the soul in silence sits
  And deigns not to complain.
Your royal ghosts, O, woodland kings!
  They reign in me at will,
And bid me, with imperial pride,
  To suffer, and be still.

They do not teach, when smote, to turn
   And give the other cheek;
Alas, O lordly ancestors!
   Ye were not over-meek:
Too much of eagle in your souls,
   Too little of the dove,
My heritage though rich in hate,
   Is poor enough in love!

We Met and Parted.

WE met and parted — only met but once,
   And then we parted. God had willed it so.
We looked within each other's eyes, and saw
Our pictures deep within each other's eyes,
And felt them each upon the other's heart.
We shivered, and we wept, and spoke of griefs
That but belonged to others: and we talked
About the woes of others — meaning ours —
Sorrows that came but of our having met,
And knowing we must part. And did we part?
Was that farewell a parting? It may be;
And yet I think it was not — I have been
Beside thee and around thee through the years
That cast their shadows back on that adieu,

And all the angels who have seen my heart
Have found a being that was still of earth
Upon its holiest altar there enshrined;
And yet they could not chide, for thou wert there:
And well enough the blessed angels knew
That nought that was not pure as pearl could come
And enter, where thy image barred the gate.
Who thinks that silence, and a thousand hills,
And years, and oceans, can avail to keep
Souls that have kissed and mingled, far apart?
They have not severed ours; they never may.
Though nought but Death can join us hand in
    hand,
There's Death enough in Life to join our hearts;
And faith enough in the sweet Life to come
Have we, to know that on the other shore
We two shall stand — two beings with one soul,
One wedded soul — as if we thus had lived,
And walked the selfsame pathway here on Earth.

Beat to her Pulses Sweet.

BEAT to her pulses sweet
  Winds of the summer night!
Creep to her bosom deep,
  Silvery streams of light!
Blow, with a lullaby low,
  Airs of the midnight still;
Come, with a murmuring hum,
  Roll of the rippling rill!
Float to her snowy throat,
  Breath of the budding flowers!
Faint to her sweet complaint,
  Damps of the dewy hours!
Meet in her heart, each sweet
  That the Earth or air has known!
Rest in her beautiful breast,
  Beautiful dreams, alone.

Eva.

Can a bird with wounded wing,
  Above the branches soar?
Can a mother gaily sing,
  When the grass is withered o'er
  A little heart, that bore
  Her own heart to the shore,
Where angel-babies meet,
And play at Jesus' feet,
  And creep the golden floor?

Through earth, forevermore,
I see an open door,
  Beyond the cloudy sleet,
  Where my dear baby's feet
Have walked the path before.
I see her beckon from the other shore;
  I listen as I dream,
That I am sailing softly o'er,
  The ripple of Life's stream.

What should I sing for now,
When her fair lily brow
Is glorified and white,
Under a crown of light?

I may not sing nor weep
Above her, in her sleep,
For the sweet Angels keep,
Kindly, the flowers they reap,
And they will guard my bud,
In her pure babyhood,
Until I go to her,
A chastened worshipper,
To press her angel face,
To my fond heart's embrace.

Why should I sing ere then?
I will sing gladly, when
My fettered soul shall rise,
From this dim world of sighs,
To the sweet upper skies,
To meet my darling's eyes,
And feel her downy head
  Upon my heart once more,
For oh! she is not dead!
  She only went before.

Too Late.

WHY art thou here, sweet bird,
    Beneath the wintry stars?
I questioned, while I heard
A withered briar stirred
    Against my window bars.
Bird of the drooping wing,
    A sweetly-moaning mouth,
    Thou shouldst be singing South.
What hope or love could bring
    Thy little straying feet,
    From leaves and roses sweet,
To press the chilly snow,
And feel the cold winds blow,
    And stem the wintry sleet?
And the bird answered, "Well, I know,
Another flower will never grow
So beautiful as that which sprung
    From out a little sod,
Where lay a flower that faded young
    To blossom up with God.
I saw it slowly bud and bloom
Above that angel-baby's tomb;
It was a clover, pure and white,
    The sweetest and the best

That ever opened to the light
  Above a baby's breast.
The robin called me, day by day,
  With sweet and wooing sound;
What cared I, while my darling lay,
  Sweet'ning the hallowed ground?
I waited but to see it die —
  It had no other mate —
And then the birds had wandered by
To love beneath a Southern sky,
  Alas! for me too late!"

Lulu Bell.

ANGELS stoop to whisper,
  When the winds are low,
O'er our little lisper,
  In her dress of snow;
With her tresses straying
  O'er the pillow white,
And the dimples playing
  Like a wave of light,
Or a halo raying
O'er an angel praying
  In the baby's sight.

As she lay, a dreaming,
  O'er her features fell
  Glory, like a spell,
And a seraph, seeming,
  Talked with LULU BELL!

Fairer than the blushes
  "When the day is born;
Sweeter than the thrushes
  In the scented thorn
Frailer than the rushes
  By the marshy dell;
Bright as beauty's flushes
  Is our LULU BELL!

  LULU BELL!
  Sweetly swell
Seas of crystal love,
From the overflowing well,
  Where a little dove,
Fluttering to a mother's breast,
Folds its snowy wings to rest.

May thy holy love abide
Till her heart is glorified,
By the silver light of years
Drifted over smiles and tears,
Over shadows, over woes,
To a haven of repose.

Darling! may'st thou ever rest,
In the sweetly-sheltered nest
Of a mother's faithful breast.
Shadow-clouds will curl above thee,
But if there is one to love thee —
One soft hand to cover over,
Thistles, in the fragrant clover,
Crushing all beside the sweet
From the pathway of thy feet,
Then, indeed, thy lot is well,
Little, gentle LULU BELL!

Bella Dowe.

GENTLE Maiden!
  Over-shaden
 By thy sunny smiles, as sweet
As the lily, interbraiden
 With the morning's dewy feet.
Up it springs, in crystal glory,
Whispers out its tender story,
 And the breezes lift it up,
 From its over-bending cup;
Loving, fragrant, holy thing,
For thy heart an offering —
 Lily! thus I liken thou,
 Unto gentle, BELLA DOWE.

BELLA DOWE!
List the vow
That I make to thee!
Ere the lilies droop again,
Underneath the summer rain,
  I shall cease to be;
And I vow thee by the blowing
  Of the lily bell so white,
That my love, forever flowing
  O'er thee, like a stream of light,
Shall flow ever, as to-night.

  I am going,
    Where the glowing,
Of diviner waters roll,
While a bud of hope is blowing
  Fragrantly, within my soul;
  It is this: Oh, BELLA DOWE!
When the grass is o'er me growing,
Thou wilt feel my love is flowing
  Softly unto thee, as now.

Loving BELLA! gentle BELLA!
Summer breezes! kindly tell her,
When the dust is on my brow,
How I love her, BELLA DOWE.

Sweet Bessie Gray.

MOTHER! I love sweet Bessie Gray
    Better than all the girls;
She is so gentle in her play,
    And has such pretty curls,

And every blessed morn, she sings
    Together with the birds:
I think that she has hidden wings,
    That flutter 'neath her words;

For I have heard a little sound
    Fill her sweet pauses out;
Perhaps, the angels were around,
    And, wondering, stayed about.

I cannot find in all my books,
    Her words, nor yet their tune;
So like the ripple of the brooks,
    Under the stars, in June.

Dear Allie Ray has hazel eyes.
    That speak their own sweet praise;
And Sue's, are like the summer skies,
    But not like Bessie Gray's.

HEART-BREATHINGS.

Sweet Bessie Gray's are like the night,
  So calm, and dark, and deep;
With a soul-star, to make the light —
  Mother! why should she weep?

For all the violets unfold,
  When her soft hands they see;
They long to wither in her hold,
  And yet, they hide from me.

The dew-drop, in the rose's heart,
  The tears, in Bessie's eyes,
Were shaken down, but fell apart,
  From flower-buds, in the skies.

Heart-Breathings.

PRESS my cold hand closer, dearest,
  To your warm heart, while I weep;
I would feel your breath the nearest
  On my lips, and o'er my sleep.
    Bend above me,
    Love, and love me,
Sing me to a slumber deep.

I should sleep, without your singing,
　　I could love, without your mouth;
For the breezes would be bringing
　　Songs and odors from the South;

Odors, they had stolen, blowing
　　O'er the sweetness of your lips;
Music, they had learned, in knowing
　　Your sweet spirit's fellowships.

I could rest, without your pressing
　　My cold hands against your heart;
But, without your murmured blessing,
　　I could never hence depart.

I could never go up yonder,
　　Through the pearly gates above,
Without smiles a little fonder,
　　Dimpling round the lips I love,
　　　　Without feeling
　　　　The revealing
Of a hope untold,
I would carry up its sealing,
　　To the upper fold.

　　　　Gentle lover!
　　　　Weep above her;
　　She will nevermore
Call a human heart to love her.

It is well she went before.
She'll be waiting at Heaven's door,
Over, on the other shore,
Ye shall walk the golden floor,
Side by side, forevermore.

Good Night.

GOOD NIGHT? ah! no; the hour is ill
    Which severs those it should unite;
Let us remain together still,
    Then, it will be — *Good* Night!

How can I call the lone night good,
    Though thy sweet wishes wing its flight?
Be it not said, thought, understood,
    Then, it will be *Good* Night!

To hearts which near each other move,
    From evening close, to morning light,
The night is good; because, my love,
    They never *say* — Good Night!

Tossed upon Life's Heaving Ocean.

TOSSED upon Life's heaving ocean,
   Swaying to its billow's motion,
Naught care I for its commotion,
   Though the storms are black above me,
While, with her divine devotion,
   I have Mary, still, to love me.

In the midnight, when the thunder
Echoes o'er the waves, and under,
Tearing ships and hearts asunder,
   None of these can ever move me,
With so wild a thrill of wonder,
   As that Mary lives to love me.

When, from out my bosom, taking
One soft tress, that stills its aching,
And three words, that checked its breaking —
   Her — "I love you" — fondly proves me,
That my heart, a heaven is making
   In the thought, that Mary loves me.

Mary! thou art all my treasure,
Grace-note of my heart's song-measure,
Thought of all my toil and leisure;
  And my soul's deep love shall prove thee,
That thou art my only pleasure,
  And that I but live, to love thee.

I will not say Good-bye.

I WILL not say — Good-bye!
  For how can you and I
Be parted, though so wide?
We walk in soul to-day,
Who seem so far away,
And wander, side by side;
There is no sad farewell,
For those who fondly dwell
Together, heart to heart;
They cannot walk apart:
And thus, I may not say —
Farewell, dear friend, to-day.

The Alpine Lovers.

I.

In a low hut, among the Alpine ledges,
    There dwelt a hunter, and a gentle maid,
Purer than flowers upon the hawthorn hedges,
    Blossomed within the glade.

She had no treasure, save the silver arrow,
    With which her radiant tresses were confined;
Sweeter than twitterings of a summer sparrow,
    Her voice rose on the wind.

What need of treasures, while the world above her,
    Glittered with gems as in the light of God?
There dwelt a hunter, who but lived to love her,
    Up where the angels trod.

He often told her, how the dear departed
    Wandered beside him, on the giddy heights;
And well she knew, that angels, loving hearted,
    Guarded him in the nights.

She never heard, of what the world calls "fashion,"
  And never thought, of what the world might say;
Yet, loving deeds, of beautiful compassion,
  Flowered on her mountain way.

She never knew, that music needed teachers,
  But learned her warblings of the singing rills;
She thought God's mountains, his divinest preachers,
  His holiest shrines, His hills!

The incense of her loving heart's devotion,
  Rose little higher than her hunter's cot;
She thought the spring of Love's auroral ocean,
  Welled from one mountain spot.

The summer came, and brought its Alpine roses,
  The hunter journeyed with an angel-guide;
And wandered forth to where the Earth-land closes,
  Nor left the angel's side.

II.

The swallows, up from the summer hedges,
  And hop across the threshold of the cot —
The hunter's cot, among the Alpine ledges —
  Singing, "Forget me not."

Go to the world, and sing about forgetting;
  O little birds! they need your lesson there—
Not to the maid, whose sun of life is setting
  Under her silver hair—

Who, through long days, and starless nights of sorrow,
  Watches forever, for the twilight tide—
The hour, that brings her, with-each coming morrow,
  Her hunter-boy, who died.

He comes, a spirit, in the twilights lonely,
  And smooths her tresses, noting not their hue;
He takes her withered hand—he loved her, only,
  And faithfully, and true.

The peasants whisper, that the hut is haunted,
  And that a wizard-vine is round the door;
They say the maiden dwells, as if enchanted,
  With one, who is no more.

I'm Dying, Comrade

I THINK I'm dying, comrade,
    The day is growing dark;
And that is not the bob-o-link,
    Nor yet the meadow-lark:
It cannot be the distant drum;
    It cannot be the fife,
For why should drum, or bob-o-link,
    Be calling me from life?

I do not think I'm wounded;
    I cannot feel a pain;
And yet I've fallen, comrade,
    Never to rise again.
The last that I remember,
    We charged upon the foe;
I heard a sound of victory,
    And that is all I know.

I think we must have conquered,
    For all last night it seemed
That I was up in Paradise —
    Among the blest, it seemed.

I'M DYING, COMRADE.

And there, beside the Throne of God,
   I saw a banner wave,
The good old Stars and Stripes, my boy,
   O'er victory and the grave.

A hundred thousand soldiers
   Stood at the right of God;
And old John Brown, he stood before,
   Like Aaron with his rod:
A slave was there beside him,
   And Jesus Christ was there;
And over God, and Christ, and all,
   The banner waved in air.

And now I'm dying, comrade,
   And there is old John Brown
A standing at the Golden Gate,
   And holding me a crown.
I do not hear the bob-o-link,
   Nor yet the drum and fife;
I only know the voice of God
   Is calling me from life.

The Lord will Make it Good.

WHAT need of the muffled music's din?
    What need of the burial rite?
Dig them a hole, and hustle them in,
    Anywhere, out of our sight.

What if they won us a glorious day?
    Was'nt it honor enough
For niggers to die in the selfsame way
    As men of a nobler stuff?

"Men of a nobler stuff," you say,
    That is for Christ to decide,
When he calls the muster-roll to-day,
    Over the other side.

What, if the land of shadows had thrown
    A darkness o'er some of the faces,
The black and the white, in heaven, are known
    Alone by the spirit's graces.

Jesus is never going to ask
    What was your color, below?
It matters him not, if the earthly mask
    Were black, or as white as snow.

THE LORD WILL MAKE IT GOOD.

Jesus will look at the Patriot's heart,
   And in heaven, it is understood,
Though the War Department pays but part,
   That the Lord will make it good.

What, if your grave is a wretched hole?
   What, if your color be that of night?
The robes of the Patriot soldier's soul,
   Are woven out of the inner light.

All the same, be you black or white,
   All the same, on the other strand;
Live and die for the regal Right,
   For God and the Right and the Fatherland.

The darkest night has the brightest stars,
   And ever the brightest dawning;
And a voice, up over his prison bars,
   Is bidding the slave — "good morning."

The prison "bars" are tumbling in,
   As they speak to one another;
Christ above, and the slave within,
While the nations shake with a jar and din,
As if to listen, alone, were sin
   To Christ's sweet call of — "brother."

I saw Thee from Afar.

IN the deep stillness of the heaven above me,
    I saw thee from afar,
Nor deemed that thou could'st ever stoop to love me,
    Thou radiant morning star!

I felt thee in the silence of the even,
    Thy presence, like a rhyme,
Thou melody from out the smiling heaven!
    Escaped before thy time.

Thou grace-note, shaken by the wings of angels
    From off the golden lyres!
Thou incense of a seraph's sweet evangels!
    Thou flame of heavenly fires!

Thou beauty and thou glory! ever trailing
    Streams of celestial light,
In thy pure pathway, up beyond our hailing,
    And far beyond our sight;

What am I, that from out thy splendor bending
    Thou hast looked kindly down,
And to my heart so graciously art lending
    Thy white love for a crown?

Our Little Bird of Paradise.

IN our hearts a baby bird,
  By her wordless warbling, stirred
Melody by angels heard.

Stooping from the starry skies,
Looking in her laughing eyes,
They beheld, with sweet surprise,

Little cherubs, pure and white,
Lying in their liquid light,
Swimming in their saintly sight.

Airs of Aiden seemed to float
Softly round her snowy throat,
While the blessed angels wrote —

Bird of Paradise, we moan
That thy wandering wings have flown
From the sweet celestial Throne.

And the angels fluttered round,
Singing inly without sound,
"The lost lamb of heaven is found."

And the mother, little knowing,
That her bosom's bud was growing,
Only for a sweeter blowing,

Heard not, in the creeping calm,
Brooding with its blessed balm,
The soft swelling of a psalm,

By whose sound, the little flower
Opened, to the magic power
Of the music's swelling shower.

When the clouds of heaven uncurl,
We can see our little girl,
Beautiful, and pure as pearl,

Looking on us, and we know
Though the nests be filled with snow,
Whence the little birdlings go,

That they flit in fairer groves,
Watching o'er their earthly loves,
Seraph-winged, celestial doves.

To William Cullen Bryant,

ON HIS SEVENTIETH BIRTHDAY, NOV. 3, 1864.

NOT from the cultured gardens,
 and not from the daisied sod,
Do I bring my little offering,
 but down from the hills of God —
Down from the crystal mountains,
 where never a flower was sown,
Save the flower that the Lord has planted.*
 in sight of the Great White Throne.

From over the nests of the eagles,
 and under the Angels' feet,
Where the opal airs of·summer
 and the winds of winter meet,

---

* The blossom of *Edelweiss* presented Mr. Bryant was gathered upon an Alpine mountain in Switzerland, nearly eleven thousand feet above the level of the sea. It grows only upon the snow mountains, and is held in great veneration by the hunters. It is the first offering an Alpine lover brings to the idol of his heart, and is believed to blossom only for sinless maidens, Poets, Saints, and the truly good. The Alpineers tell us that it will wither and die if a bad man but look upon it.

A flower I bring — an offering
   from the snow-hill's silver crest,
And leave sweet songs, and laurel crowns,
   and Earth-flowers, for the rest.

The Alpine hunters tell us,
   that when a Poet dies,
God meets him at the Golden Gate,
   crowned with the *Edelweiss*.
But only those who've worshipped Him
   in singing Nature's praise,
And walked beside Him on the hills,
   and through Life's lowly ways.

O, King of Nature's Songsters!
   and thus I bring to thee,
This blossom from the Alpine hills —
   the glorious and Free;
That when the Angels bid thee pause,
   where oft thy soul has trod
To crown thee on the mountain tops,
   upon thy way to God,

That thou may'st recognize the flower
   as one, while yet below,
And walking in the Earthly ways,
   thou still had'st learned to know.

Thus, from no cultured garden,
  and not from the daisied sod,
Do I bring my little offering
  but down from the hills of God.

Angels! Lead Her Lightly.

ANGELS! lead her lightly
  Up the heavenly stairs,
Never soul so slightly
  Needed earthly prayers.

Leave her where the glory
  Of His shadow falls,
There to tell her story
  When her Saviour calls.

She will whisper faintly
  Of her sin and shame,
When in accents saintly
  Jesus calls her name,

"Mary!" and the Angels,
  Singing round the Throne,
Cease their sweet evangels
  At that tender tone.

All the saints in Aiden
    That for joy were dumb,
Echo round the maiden,
    Jesus' gentle, " Come."

The Old Year.

COULD the dear and dead old year,
    Arise from out the past,
And bring again his sunshine here,
    And bid its glory last —
We would not lure him back again,
With all the midnights and the rain,
E'en though his twilight tints were sweet,
And rosy his auroral feet —
Although his dews were pure and clear,
And all his blessed birds were dear,
For there were ravens in the dark,
Who sang not like the morning lark,
But croaked with visage dark and grim,
A symphony to her sweet hymn;—
And there were ravens of the heart
Who, looking forward, saw the dart.

That turned our morning into night,
Who knew our roses hid a blight.
Oh no, we would not lure him back.
With all the shadows on his track.

The New Year.

WELCOME to the prince of Earth,
    Regal Conqueror by birth,
Kindly deal with us and ours,
Lead us over beds of flowers,
And beside Life's limpid streams,
Where the soul's sweet sunshine beams.
Lead us not into the dark,
Where no singing wren nor lark
Wakes the morning with his mirth,
Glorifying Life and Earth,
Sweetening all the air above,
With the fragrance of its love.
By the holy water flood,
Sanctified with sacred blood,
Lead us, like the lambs of Him,
In whose light the planets swim,
Nearer to the heavenly rest,
On our Father's faithful breast.

Our Souls leap over the Years.

OUR Souls leap over the years,
    And we measure them not by days,
We count by the tears, by the hopes and fears,
    That flicker in Life's highways.

We count by the throbs of the bounding heart,
    By its beautiful budding dreams,
By the joys that start as its buds unpart,
    And deluge our heart like streams.

We count by the smothered sobs that rise
    To the breast like the blight on flowers,
By the soul's low sighs, and the sad good-byes,
    And the sound of the Autumn showers —

By the sound of the pattering drops that fall
    On the heart when its leaves are sere,
By the robin's call, when his roses all
    Are asleep with the dead old year.

We count by the roses sweet,
    That withered and dropped from our hold,
And above the sleet, by the Angel feet,
    That walk in the streets of gold.

We count by the beautiful hands that pressed
    The sweet to the cup of gall,
By the gentle breast, with its saintly rest,
    Where the sifting snow-flakes fall —

By the loved on whom the snow
    Is falling in crystal flakes,
By the plaintive flow of the anthem low,
    That the heart breathes when it breaks —

By the hills we have heaped so high,
    Of passion, of hate, and of scorn,
To the tinted sky, as the Angels sigh
    For the sin of the earthly born.

We count by the days misspent,
    By the good which we might have done,
By the lute-strings bent, and the songs unlent,
    That we clasped to our hearts *for one* —

By the beautiful golden strings
    Of the glittering harp, whose tune
An echo brings o'er the folded wings
    Of the birds that sang in June —

Of the Spirit-birds, whose flight
    Was over beyond the stars,
Whose soft wings white, were dipped in light,
    Whose deeds were the crystal cars,

By whose radiant wheels they swept,
   Far over the Earthly strand —
For the tears we wept, for the loved who stepped
   Across to the Better Land.

We measure our years by the beat
   Of our fluttering hearts, and wait
For a blessed seat, with the sainted sweet,
   Who sit by the jasper gate —

By the trust in the love we press
   To our hearts, like a garment white,
By the lips which bless, with a mute caress,
   Our own, with a kiss of light —

By the hands we would clasp again,
   By the loved who will love no more,
By our souls refrain, while the spirit rain,
   Is flooding the life-cup o'er.

Our souls leap over the years,
   And we measure them not by days —
We count by the tears, by the hopes and fears,
   That flicker in Life's highways.

Thine at Last.

I FAIN would send thee, dearest,
   One little token-flower,
But the flowers have lost their sweetness,
   And my love has lost its power.
Oh, tell me there is yet one chord
   Unbroken still the same,
In thy dear heart, that answereth,
   Though faintly, to my name,
And I will give the wooing air,
   And loving breeze, a tone,
And when they kiss thy golden hair,
   It is my lips, mine own.

Oh, dearest, come to me!
The blessed angels see
My yearning heart o'erleap
Its doubts and shadows deep,
And nestle down by thee.
Come in the silent night,
With thy sweet soul so white,
   And say to mine,
Life is not life nor light,
My heart has no delight,
   Unshared with thine.

The little snowdrops cling
  In silence to the stem,
An offering I bring
  Thy gentle heart of them.
The snow is dropping, Love,
  In pure and pearly flakes,
My weary heart above,
  Oh, God! it breaks, it breaks!—

I live, I live, I wake,
  The snow is melting fast,
For thy dear smile's sweet sake,
  And I am thine at last.

Allie Grey.

THE snow was white around the home
  Of gentle Allie Grey,
And she, upon her little bed
  In silent sorrow lay;

The mother sat beside her child,
  And kissed her chilly cheek,
But oh, she was so still and cold,
  She scarce could smile, or speak.

ALLIE GREY.

The angels came from Paradise
  And told sweet Allie Grey,
That neither storm, nor snow, nor ice,
  Beyond the Earth-land lay.

And Allie whispered very low,
  O, tell me, mother sweet,
And will the angels give me shoes
  To warm my little feet?

And can I sit the whole day long
  Beside the fire, at play?
They said it was a sunny land
  In Heaven, so far away.

And shall I gather violets
  Beneath the warming sky?
But I will shut my eyes, mamma,
  And try to sleep and die.

And then the Angels came again,
  With songs so soft and low,
And took her up beyond the land
  Of chilly winds and snow.

The Swiss Peasant Woman's Offering to the Sanitary Fair.*

IT is'nt much, Herr Consul, that I have brought to-day,
But you're welcome to the little, as to the flowers of May;
There is'nt much upon the Alps except the pines and flowers,
The sunshine and the sparkling dew, and all the singing showers;

---

* Of all the gifts received for this Fair, perhaps the most touching is that given by an Alpine peasant woman in Zurich, Switzerland — a tiny book of pressed Alpine flowers, together with a simple wooden wine-cup that formerly belonged to her son, now a soldier in the Union Army. On presenting the cup and the little book of flowers, the good old woman took a bottle of red Switzer wine from her pocket, and filling the cup, handed it to the Consul, and then drank herself, saying: — "There's a health and a greeting to America; God bless my boy's new Fatherland." "God bless it," replied the Consul, "and Switzerland too." The old woman thanked him with tears in her eyes, and went away, leaving her boy's cup and the Alpine blossoms behind her.

An American lady, residing in Zurich, being at the rooms of the American Consulate, when the poor woman came trembling in with her gift, wrote the following impromptu lines for the donor, and placed them in the cup. — *New York Tribune.*

TO THE SANITARY FAIR.

But I couldn't catch the sunshine, nor bottle up
    the dew,
And the pine nuts of the Alpine hills are not for
    such as you;
And so I brought the blossoms that bloom upon
    the hills,
And open on the sunny banks beside the glacier rills;
If you think them worth the sending, I shall indeed
    be glad,
There may be one who'll buy them — perhaps a
    Switzer lad.
My boy is in America, you may have seen him
    there,
You'd know him by his mountain tone, and by his
    golden hair;
His voice was like an Alpine horn, so clear its
    crystal notes,
'T was like the music of a song to hear him call his
    goats;
The boy was gentle as a kid, and yet as full of fire,
And dauntless, as that royal bird, the Alpine *lum-
    mergeir;* —
It is'nt much, Herr Consul, that such as I can bring,
But here is Hiery's wine-cup — a little simple
    thing —
A Switzer wine-cup fragrant still with all the sweet
    perfumes
Of violets, and forget-me-nots, and choicest Alpine
    blooms;

So take the cup, Herr Consul, and take the Alpine
    flowers,
For they may mind some Switzer lad of happy
    by-gone hours.
Fill up the little Switzer cup with sparkling Switzer
    wie; *
A high health to America, the Country of the
    Free!

Jack and Jim, Comrades, who fell at the Battle of Fort Fisher.

I KNOW not what's the matter, Jack,
    but all the livelong day
I've thought about the meadow brook,
    by which we used to play;
I've seemed to hear its singing sound,
    and see the pebbles gleam,
As if the very stars of heaven
    were shining from the stream.

I never noticed how they shone,
    until one May-day morn,
When you and I were sowing in
    the widow Johnson's corn.

---

* "*Wie*" — the Swiss peasant word for wine.

O, Jack! if you could know my heart,
   you wouldn't think me weak,
Not even though the blinding tears
   are falling as I speak.

As we were planting there the corn
   that morning in the May,
Perhaps you don't remember it,
   but Mary came that way;
She waded right across the brook,
   with feet as bare as ours,
And ever since, the pebbles shine,
   and gems are on the flowers!

I wished I were the butter-cup
   she crushed beneath her feet —
You may not like the fancy, Jack,
   and yet it seems so sweet.
O, Jack! she came along that way,
   and yet I dared not look
To see her standing on the bank,
   and smiling in the brook,

Bear with me yet a little while,
   though foolish it may seem,
To you who never loved her, Jack,
   or kissed her in your dream.

I think the love was given to me
   when God he gave me life,
For when not more than four years old,
   I played she was my wife.

'T was I who made the little sled
   whereon she loved to slide,
And the wagon, from a raisin box,
   in which she used to ride —
The box I had of Nathan Jones,
   who kept the village store,
And I whittled out the little wheels,
   Indeed, 't was quite a chore.

The fellows all are fast asleep,
   and you mustn't keep awake,
For the battle of to-morrow
   begins with morning's break;
'T was wrong of me to talk to you
   so long into the night,
But we may never meet again
   after the morrow's fight.

If there's any word you want to send,
   't were better not to wait,
For if you should'nt speak to night,
   it might then be too late.

What shall I tell the folks at home,
  if you, dear boy, should die?
O, Jack! I never dreamed that aught
  could sever you and I.

We're nearer now, by far, dear Jim,
  than even you suppose;
We've shared each other's joys in life,
  and felt each other's woes —
I cannot talk; but here's a note
  I finished as you came,
Take it, and give it, if I fall,
  within, you'll find the name.

Sweet Mary Gray, the psalm to-day
  must other voices sing,
For all the song within your soul
  is out upon the wing;
It is as if the winds of heaven
  had wafted every tone
Up to the sainted listeners,
  beside the Golden Throne.

Why press your hands upon your heart
  with lowly bended head?
They hide away from glare of day
  a letter, stained with red.

O, Mary Gray, you can but pray,
  and He who feeds the bird,
Will give you calm, and send you balm,
  as written in His Word.

O, Jack and Jim! ye never thought
  to lie together there,
Within the dear old meeting-house
  with roses in your hair —
With blossoms on your bosoms,
  and the old Flag over each,
And Elder Mills within the desk,
  sobbing too much to preach.

Alas, poor boys! ye both have dreamed
  of standing there one day,
With roses, and with orange-flowers,
  and with sweet Mary Gray.
O, Jim! a blessed thing for you,
  this sleep, without a dream —
God's ways are always merciful
  however hard they seem.

It matters little now, dear Jack,
  that gentle Mary Gray
Has smoothed your clustering golden curls,
  and kissed your cheek to-day;

'T is all the same to you in heaven,
   and may be too, to Jim —
God comforts those, sweet Mary Gray,
   who put their trust in Him.

Good Friday,
AT THE ISLE OF UFNAU.*

SILENCE, and hush profound
   Brood in the air around,
     The Saviour sleeps.
Even the bird's sweet notes
Are hushed within their throats,
   And the soft south wind keeps
   Among the hills, and weeps.
The still and fragrant air
Is eloquent with prayer.
     The Saviour sleeps.

---

* Written at the Isle of Ufnau in Lake Zurich, Switzerland. This beautiful island, which contains one dwelling-house, and three churches, is distinguished as being the death and burial-place of Ulrich Van Hutten, the first singer of German Liberty. The Monks of Einsiedeln, who are the proprietors of the island, hold services in its churches during the season of Lent.

O, little ones and weak!
Let the sweet stillness speak
   Of sweetest calm —
Sweeter than timbrel's tone,
Or harp's melodious moan.
   Or murmuring psalm.
Watch, and in silence pray,
They will not come to-day
And roll the stone away —
   The Saviour sleeps.

The Dead Boy.

I LOOK along the floor —
  I see a precious store
Of tiny, half-worn toys,
Such as all little boys
So love to treasure up —
Here is his silver cup,
And here, a ragged book —
Blinded by tears I look!
The cup is standing still
Upon the window sill,
Just as he placed it there,
After his evening prayer —
Before he went to bed,
   And laid him down to sleep.

THE DEAD BOY.

"Mother," the darling said,
  "Will God the kitten keep
And watch it in the night,
    If it be good and mild,
    Just like a pleasant child,
And does'nt scratch nor bite?"
Alas, the kitten plays
Along the garden ways,
But all alone to-day.
And I must put away
Each little blessed toy,
Because my angel boy
Will want them nevermore;
For all his plays are o'er.
How can I lay aside
  The bell he loved to ring?
Must these knots be untied
  In every dangling string?
There are his little shoes
  Beneath his cherished chair,
He never more may loose
  One of the precious pair;
They are too worn to use,
  But who on earth will care?
Are they not dearer still,
  Now that his little feet
Have climbed the heavenly hill,
  And walked the golden street?

The Twin Baby Sleepers.*

LYING 'neath the golden gleaming
   Of the blessed evening star,
Little sleepers! ye are seeming
With its glory softly teeming,
Beaming through your gentle dreaming
   From the beautiful afar;
     Softly sleeping,
     In the keeping
   Of the angels from afar.

Those dear little hands are holding
In a clasping, close enfolding,
One another's tiny palms,
Breathing, blest, embodied psalms!
     How completely,
     And how sweetly
Love is locked in your still arms!

Mother of the little sleepers!
   Looking upward through the dark,
Know there are no weary weepers
   Up beyond the singing lark.

---

* Children of a beautiful young mother, who is a widow.

> The Supernal
> One, Eternal,
> Is the Helmsman of Life's barque,
> Kindly guiding
> Its still gliding,
> And its tossing, in the dark.

"It might have been."

I WOULD have asked one thing, love,
  One dearest thing of thee —
That the name you gave another
  You had only given to me.

Yet, in the fair hereafter,
  It will be all the same —
I shall love to hear the Angels
  Calling my Angel name.

For I know the magic music
  Of thy name will then be mine,
And my heart will beat the time, love,
  To the melody of thine.

Song of the Rhine.

I HEAR the ripple of the Rhine,
  Under the stars, at the day's decline,
And to my heart when night is still,
Its music brings a magic thrill.

The linden leaves are leaning low,
The blushing roses faintly blow,
And royally around the Rhine,
Cluster Maria's hopes, and mine.

She hears with me its ripple low,
  And wonders if our lives will glide
In half so musical a flow,
  Together, by its singing side.

O, God! I shiver with afright,
  My star of life has ceased to shine;
A shadow swims around the night!
  And — it is raining in the Rhine.

Let the Angels be my Guide.

AS I kneel before the throne,
   Speaking in the softest tone,
Only unto God alone,
Floods of crimson swiftly roll
Over face, and heart, and soul,
Into being sweetly stirred
By the music of a word,
Lightly murmured though it be,
Father! only unto Thee.

Jesus — whisper I, and weep —
There is one across the deep;
Send him angels in his sleep,
" Watch and ward o'er him to keep."
There is something yet beside,
(With the angels as a guide,)
I would ask thee if I may —
Something else for which I pray;
Let the angels be my guide.

There is one across the deep,
Moaning in his weary sleep;
May I go, with a noiseless tread —
Sit in dreams beside his bed —

Lay within his fevered palm
Cooling hands with touch of balm,
Wooing quietude and calm.
Little matter if he knows
Whence the healing influence flows,
Lulling him to soft repose.

Yet, alas! whene'er I go,
It would still be sweet to know
That he felt my presence round him,
Knew whose loving arms enwound him,
And whose eyes and heart were waking;
Whose poor heart was almost breaking
With its anguished love and fears —
Thus I fall asleep in tears;
Thus I dream away the years.

M289867

THE UNIVERSITY OF CALIFORNIA LIBRARY

www.ingramcontent.com/pod-product-compliance
Lightning Source LLC
Chambersburg PA
CBHW031402160426
43196CB00007B/867